THE COMING ISLAMIC INVASION OF ISRAEL

MARK HITCHCOCK

Multnomah®Publishers *Sisters, Oregon*

THE COMING ISLAMIC INVASION OF ISRAEL
published by Multnomah Publishers, Inc.
© 2002 by Mark Hitchcock

International Standard Book Number: 1-59052-048-3

Cover design by Kirk DouPonce/UDG DesignWorks
Cover images by Corbis, Photodisk, and PhotoSpin

Unless otherwise indicated, Scripture quotations are from:
New American Standard Bible® © 1960, 1977, 1995
by the Lockman Foundation. Used by permission.

Other Scripture quotations:
Holy Bible, New Living Translation (NLT) © 1996.
Used by permission of Tyndale House Publishers, Inc. All rights reserved.
The American Standard Bible (ASV) © 1901
The Holy Bible, King James Version (KJV)
The Holy Bible, New International Version (NIV) © 1973, 1984 by International
Bible Society, used by permission of Zondervan Publishing House

Multnomah is a trademark of Multnomah Publishers, Inc.,
and is registered in the U.S. Patent and Trademark Office.
The colophon is a trademark of Multnomah Publishers, Inc.

Printed in the United States of America

For information:
MULTNOMAH PUBLISHERS, INC.•POST OFFICE BOX 1720
SISTERS, OREGON 97759

Library of Congress Cataloging-in-Publication Data
Hitchcock, Mark.
    The coming Islamic invasion of Israel / Mark Hitchcock.
        p. cm.
Includes bibliographical references.
    ISBN 1-59052-048-3 (pbk.)
    1. Bible. O.T. Ezekiel XXXVIII-XXXIX--Prophecies--Israel. 2. Bible. O.T. Ezekiel
XXXVIII-XXXIX--Prophecies--Islamic countries. 3. Bible. O.T. Ezekiel XXXVIII-
XXXIX--Prophecies--Russia (Federation) I. Title.
    BS1545.6.P26 H58 2002
    236'.9--dc21   2002006630

02 03 04 05 06 07 08—10 9 8 7 6 5 4 3 2 1 0

DEDICATION

To Dr. Harold L. Willmington,
my mentor, encourager, and friend.
The times we spend together talking about God's
Word are some of "the best of times" in my life.
Thank you for your consistent example
of faithfulness to God and His Word.
You're a modern Apollos—
"an eloquent man… mighty in the Scriptures"
(Acts 18:24).

CONTENTS

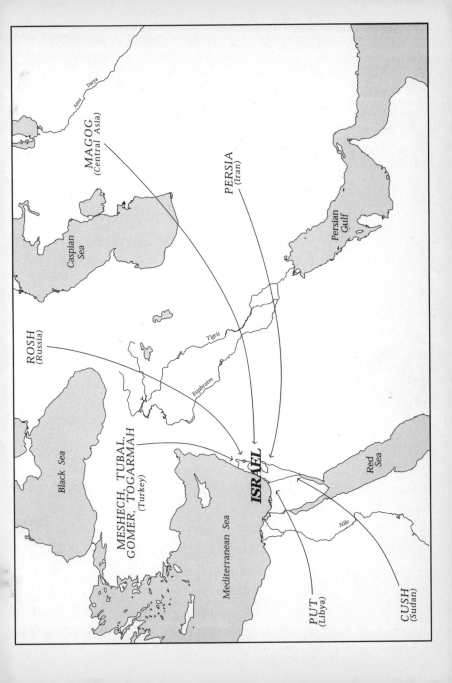

INTRODUCTION

O f all the end-time prophecies in the Bible, one in particular continues to grip me.

It is the account of a future invasion of Israel led by Russia and joined by a vast horde of Islamic nations on all sides. Ezekiel 38–39 describes this key event of the end times, which is often called the Battle of Gog and Magog.

In the wake of the September 11 attack against the United States by Islamic terrorists, hosts of books about Islam have been hitting the shelves in bookstores across America. From these many titles, we've been learning a great deal that we didn't know about Islam's past and present.

And frankly, the picture that emerges isn't very pretty.

As much as some try to put a positive spin on Islam and its storied history and teachings, the hard truth really can't be hidden: Radical Islam is especially hostile toward Judaism and Christianity.

While many of these books have been very helpful, few seem willing to touch on the *future* of Islam. The reason is really quite simple. No one on earth knows the future! But there is one book that tells us some amazing things about the future of Islam, and that book, of course, is the Bible. Only the author of Scripture, the true and living God, can accurately tell the future.

The first book of this Signs of the Times series, *What on Earth Is Going On?,* included a chapter entitled "The Coming Islamic Invasion of Israel." In light of current events, I believe it is crucial for believers to grasp what God's Word says about this coming event predicted in the Bible. In one short chapter, however, I really couldn't go into much detail about this future

Islamic invasion. The folks at Multnomah agreed and encouraged me to expand that chapter into an entire book with the same title…the book you now hold in your hands.

At the outset, I want every reader to know that I do not hate followers of Islam. Nothing in this book is intended to imply or convey such an attitude. God loves sinners no matter what their particular ethnic background is. He loves them regardless of what their particular errors, sins, or false beliefs might be. God is gracious and patient. He is never in a hurry to judge.

But someday He *will* judge.

And when He pours out His wrath, it will be not just against Muslims, but against all who have rejected the free gift of salvation through His Son, Jesus Christ.

I have visited Turkey and Jordan on several occasions on study and mission trips and have a great and growing desire to see the gospel of Christ reach people who have been deceived by the teachings of Islam. My purpose in these pages is to simply state what I believe the Word of God says about the final invasion of Israel by a confederacy of Islamic nations. But while there is still time, we should do all we can to spread the gospel to Muslims in our own country and abroad.

In this book I am going to assume that the reader has at least a basic knowledge of a few key events in the end times. But just to make sure you understand these events at the outset, let's do a brief review and define a few key terms that you will see sprinkled throughout the coming chapters.

THE RAPTURE OF THE CHURCH TO HEAVEN

This next event on God's prophetic timetable will occur when all who have personally trusted in Jesus Christ as their Savior, the living and the dead, will be caught up to meet the Lord in the air and go with Him back up to heaven. At least seven years later, these believers will return with Him to earth at His second coming (see John 14:1–3; 1 Corinthians 15:50–58; 1 Thessalonians 4:13–18).

THE SEVEN-YEAR TRIBULATION PERIOD

The Tribulation is the final seven years of this age. It will begin with a peace treaty between Israel and the

Antichrist and end with the second coming of Christ to earth. During this time the Lord will pour out His wrath upon the earth in successive waves of judgment. But the Lord will also pour out His grace by saving millions during this time (see Revelation 6–19).

THE THREE-AND-A-HALF-YEAR WORLD EMPIRE OF THE ANTICHRIST

During the last half of the Tribulation, the Antichrist will rule the world—politically, economically, and religiously. The entire world will give allegiance to him or suffer persecution and death (see Revelation 13:1–18).

THE CAMPAIGN OF ARMAGEDDON (WORLD WAR III)

The Campaign or War of Armageddon is the final event of the Great Tribulation. All the armies of the earth will gather to come against Israel and attempt once and for all to eradicate the Jewish people. (See Revelation 14:19–20; 16:12–16; 19:19–21.)

THE SECOND COMING
OF CHRIST TO EARTH

The climactic event of human history is the literal, physical, visible, glorious return of Jesus Christ to planet earth. He will destroy the armies of the world gathered in Israel, and set up His kingdom on earth that will last for one thousand years (see Revelation 19:11–21).

God's Blueprint for the End Times

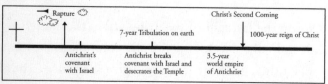

One more thing before you begin reading this book. Why not turn in your Bible to Ezekiel 38–39 and read these two incredible chapters? These two chapters of Scripture are the foundation and background for this book. Reading them first will give you a great head start on our study.

My sincere prayer is that God will use this book in your life to help you better understand what His Word says about a future all-out invasion of Israel, how current events in our world today seem to be setting the stage for this world-changing event, and how we should live our lives as we await the coming of Jesus Christ.

Maranatha!
"Our Lord, Come!"

MARK HITCHCOCK

SETTING THE STAGE

Russia and a massive Islamic alliance are going to invade Israel.

If I had made this statement sixty years ago, it would have seemed ridiculous.

First of all, there was no nation of Israel to invade!

For nineteen centuries the Jewish people had been scattered all over the world. At that very time, they were being herded together and incinerated by the millions in the Nazi houses of horror, better known as death camps. While Jews were fighting for their very survival as a people, the idea of a rebirth of their nation would have seemed like nothing more than an illusion.

Who could have imagined that a few years later they would have part of their own homeland back? At the same time, none of the Islamic nations that are so dangerous today were even blips on the international radar screen. The thought of their attacking anybody was a joke.

But it's anything but a joke today.

The world today is like a powder keg with a lighted fuse. Present conditions all over the world indicate that the fuse could burn its way to the end very soon, exploding into worldwide conflict and chaos.

THE NEW WORLD DISORDER

Not long ago on the Fox News Channel, Bill O'Reilly observed that "the world today is a more dangerous place than it's ever been." Most of us have probably thought the same thing in the past few months or years. It seems that as each day passes, the world seems to spin closer and closer to the brink. There are undoubtedly many reasons why this is true, but one that would be at the top of almost everyone's list is the meteoric rise of militant Islam.

The beginning of modern radical Islam can probably

be traced to the Iranian revolution in 1979, led by Ayatollah Khomeini. The takeover of the American embassy in Tehran and the internment of its staff are etched in the minds of all Americans.

After 1979, the Iranian revolution was exported to other nations and gained momentum in the 1980s. But a movement that was already gaining ground was rocketed forward by three strategic events from 1989 to 1991:

1. the defeat of the Soviets in Afghanistan in 1989,
2. the Gulf War in early 1991, and
3. the demise of the Soviet Union in December 1991.

Since 1991, militant Islam has literally exploded on the world scene. A recent article in *Reader's Digest* highlighted the current threat of radical Islam to Muslim countries and the world.

Modern Islam is under siege. The vast territories of Islam are now filled with radicalism, and the faith has been hijacked by those who preach that political power must be anchored in religious zeal. This is the siren song of Osama bin Laden and those who carry his banner.

Their core followers are the impoverished youth of Islam—urban, half-educated, on the run from security services in their homelands. They are drifters who stare at us in the daily newspapers, rounded up in the global hunt for terrorists. And their numbers are legion and still growing.

These militants have targeted governments in their own Muslim world, confident that a tide of Islamic fundamentalism will sweep more moderate secular rulers away.... Here's why their struggles won't end soon and what their turmoil could mean to America and the world.[1]

IT IS WRITTEN

Although the rise of militant Islam has shocked and surprised many people around the world, the God of

Scripture has not been taken off guard. Approximately 2,600 years ago, through the prophet Ezekiel, God predicted events that are strikingly foreshadowed by what we see developing before our eyes every day on the evening news.

Ezekiel 36–39 is history written beforehand. It describes the regathering of Jews to the land of Israel in the end times, followed by an all-out invasion of Israel by a massive assault force. On May 14, 1948, Israel became a nation against all odds, preparing the way for Ezekiel 38–39 to be fulfilled. As we look around today, other events are further setting the stage for Ezekiel 38–39 to come to pass exactly as God predicted.

We need to remember that God has already written the script for the end times. He is the author of the ages. Seven times in Ezekiel 38–39 we read the same words: "Thus says the Lord GOD" (38:3, 10, 14, 17; 39:1, 17, 25). Another eight times the refrain "declares the Lord GOD" appears. Obviously, God doesn't want us to miss the point: This is His word! The prediction in Ezekiel 38–39 comes directly from Him. He is the author of the script.

And He is also the director.

DIRECTED BY GOD

At the end of every movie when the credits begin to roll, one of the first items to appear is "directed by...." If Bible prophecy had a list of credits, it would read, "directed by God."

As director and producer, God is orchestrating, organizing, and overruling world events to set the stage for a drama like no other. He is making sure that all the players will be in the right place when the curtain goes up at the Rapture.

Over and over again in Ezekiel 38–39, God makes it clear that He is in charge. He says to these future invaders, "I will turn you about and put hooks into your jaws, and I will bring you out" (38:4). God pictures these invading nations as a huge crocodile that He drags out of the water. We might say that God is the original "Crocodile Hunter."

In other places, God further emphasizes again and again that He is the one who sovereignly sets the stage. "You will be summoned" (38:8), "I will bring you against My land" (38:16), "and I will turn you around, drive you on, take you up...and bring you against the mountains of Israel" (39:2).

Is God, then, violating the will of these invaders by bringing them into Israel? Not at all. They *want* to come. They "devise an evil plan," and God holds them responsible for it (38:10). Nothing in this statement is meant in any way to diminish human responsibility. The point is that God is ultimately and finally in control. He is the one who makes sure the stage is perfectly set for His great prophetic production.

God has scripted many events and participants to play a role in His prophetic production: the Antichrist, the rebuilding of the temple in Jerusalem, the reuniting of the Roman empire, and the final great War of Armageddon. One of the major events that God has scripted is the first great battle of the end times predicted in Ezekiel 38–39: the Battle of Gog and Magog.

THE PICTURE ON THE BOX

In light of all that's going on in our world today, I love to read the newspaper every morning and tune in to the cable news channels. Sometimes, however, listening to the news or reading the newspaper today can be like staring at a table covered with pieces of a jigsaw puzzle. Although so many articles and reports seem to relate to the stage setting for the end times, it can be difficult to put the pieces together.

What's the key to successfully assembling a jigsaw puzzle? The picture on the box, of course. In the same way, God's prophecies in the Bible serve as the guide, master plan, or picture on the box by which we can evaluate the many current events in our world today to see how they fit together in God's program for this world.

Ezekiel 38–39 is a key part of the picture on the box of God's master plan for history. In this book I want you to join me as we take a serious look at the details of these two chapters in God's Word. Let's see what the picture on the box looks like and then begin to evaluate how events in our world today clearly point toward what we see in these chapters.

If you were ever in beginning journalism in high school, you'll probably remember the six questions every reporter was supposed to bring to each story: who, what, when, where, why, and how. Let's use these questions to guide us through some significant points in Ezekiel 38–39.

The *where* question is easy. It's obvious we're talking about Israel—the very same piece of land that Abraham and Sarah traversed approximately four thousand years ago.

But *who* are the specific nations that will participate in this invasion (see Ezekiel 38:1–7)?

When will it happen (see Ezekiel 38:8)?

Why will they attack (see Ezekiel 38:9–12)?

What will happen in this battle (see Ezekiel 38:13–39:20)?

And finally, *how* should we personally respond?

Let's get started in the next three chapters by looking at Ezekiel 38:1–7—God's who's who of end-time nations that will invade Israel.

GOG AND MAGOG

Ezekiel doesn't waste any time. He jumps right into his amazing prophecy by introducing us to the nations that will participate in this end-time assault against Israel. His list contains ten proper names. We could call this list "God's Top-Ten Most Wanted List," because God says that He is against them and their evil plan to invade Israel (see 38:3).

About 2,600 years ago the prophet Ezekiel listed the precise alliance of nations that will invade Israel in the latter years, or end times.

And the word of the LORD came to me saying, "Son of man, set your face toward *Gog* of the land of *Magog,* the prince of *Rosh, Meshech* and *Tubal,* and prophesy against him and say, 'Thus says the Lord GOD, "Behold, I am against you, O Gog, prince of Rosh, Meshech and Tubal. I will turn you about and put hooks into your jaws, and I will bring you out, and all your army, horses and horsemen, all of them splendidly attired, a great company with buckler and shield, all of them wielding swords; *Persia, Ethiopia* and *Put* with them, all of them with shield and helmet; *Gomer* with all its troops; *Beth-togarmah* from the remote parts of the north with all it troops—many peoples with you. Be prepared, and prepare yourself, you and all your companies that are assembled about you, and be a guard for them."'" (Ezekiel 38:1–7, emphasis added)

The best place to begin in approaching a part of the Bible as complicated as Ezekiel 38–39 is to identify the nations specifically named by the prophet—

ancient geographical names of countries well known in his day but totally foreign to us now. Our task is to determine which countries inhabit these ancient lands *today*. As we identify the modern countries one by one, I think you'll be amazed.

It reads like a who's-who list of Israel's current enemies.

Gog: Public Enemy #1

The first name to appear on "God's Top-Ten Most Wanted List" is the strange name of *Gog*. In 1 Chronicles 5:4, Gog is listed as one of the descendants of Reuben, but that Gog has no relation to the Gog of Ezekiel.

There are four things we can say about Gog. *First, Gog is a person, not a place.* Ezekiel says that Gog is "of the land of Magog" and that he is the "prince of Rosh, Meshech and Tubal" (Ezekiel 38:2). This clearly identifies Gog as a ruler or prince of nations.

Second, Gog is the leader of this invasion. In Ezekiel 38–39, the name *Gog* appears eleven times, more than any other name. God directly addresses Gog on several occasions in these chapters. This leads me to conclude that Gog is the leader or key figure in this invading force.

We need to be careful not to confuse Gog with another key end-time political/military leader known as the Antichrist. The Antichrist rules the great Western confederation of nations during the first part of the Tribulation and eventually the whole world for three and a half years. Gog, however, leads a great Russian-Islamic alliance of nations in opposition to Israel and the Antichrist, as we will see later.

Gog and Antichrist are not the same person. In fact, they are rivals during the first half of the Tribulation. Gog leads his troops into Israel for the Battle of Gog and Magog; Antichrist leads his army into Israel at the very end of the Tribulation for the War of Armageddon.

Third, although Gog could be the person's name, it is probably a title—like president, Caesar, or general. Gog personifies the evil forces who gather against Israel to destroy her.

Fourth, we know that Gog is from the land of Magog and rules over Rosh, Meshech, and Tubal. To discern the precise land from which Gog arises, we must identify the land of Magog.

THE LAND OF MAGOG

Magog was the second son of Japheth, the son of Noah (see Genesis 10:2). His name appears in the Bible in 1 Chronicles 1:5, Ezekiel 38:2, and Ezekiel 39:6. Outside the Bible, the name is not found in ancient literature except by those commenting on the Bible. Magog has been identified with several ancient groups of people by biblical commentators. The most likely identification, however, is provided by the Jewish historian Josephus who said, "Magog founded the Magogians, thus named after him, but who by the Greeks are called Scythians."[2]

The ancient Scythians were a great nomadic tribe who inhabited the ancient territory from Central Asia all across the southern part of ancient Russia. The descendants of Magog were the original inhabitants of the plateau of Central Asia.

MODERN MAGOG

Today the land of Magog is inhabited by the former Soviet republics of Kazakhstan, Kyrgyzstan, Uzbekistan, Turkmenistan, Tajikistan, and possibly even northern parts of modern Afghanistan. All of these nations today have one thing in common: *Islam.* And within their borders they have a combined population of 60 million.

When the Soviet Union came crashing down in December 1991, the people of Central Asia immediately and exuberantly embraced Islam, the religion they had been forced to renounce or secretly practice for seventy-four years. Since 1991, militant Islam has been on the rise in Central Asia. Ahmed Rashid, an expert on Central Asia, says that one of the greatest threats to Central Asia today is militant Islam, primarily centered in three radical groups.

The first of these groups is known as the Islamic Renaissance Party (IRP). The second is the Islamic Movement of Uzbekistan (IMU).[3] Under its leader Juma Namangani, the IMU extended its jihad to all of Central Asia. A third even more widespread Islamic movement in Central Asia is Hizb ut-Tahrir al-Islami (HT—the Party of Islamic Liberation). This movement has declared jihad in Central Asia and is working to reunite all the Central Asian nations and ultimately the whole Muslim world.[4]

Tajikistan experienced a bloody civil war from

1992 to 1997 that had the highest number of casualties in proportion to population of any civil war in the last fifty years. The source of the civil war was a political coup by an extremist Islamic movement. Rashid says that "Central Asia is almost certain to become the new global battleground."[5]

Over the last ten years, Iran, Turkey, and Russia have each exerted influence and sought to develop closer ties to the nations of Central Asia. The Bible says that someday a great leader will come from this part of the world who will weld together a great coalition of nations to invade Israel. The developing situation in Central Asia today points toward the end-time scenario we see in Ezekiel 38.

Gog, Magog, and the Koran

To me, one of the most fascinating aspects of Ezekiel 38–39 is that Islam has its own version of the Battle of Gog and Magog, called the War of Yajuj and Majuj. In two places the Koran specifically mentions Gog and Magog (Yajuj and Majuj) by name (18:96; 21:96).

In Islamic eschatology, or teaching on the end times, ten major signs signal the approach of the end and the day of resurrection. There are various opinions about the order in which these signs take place, but in one list I have seen Gog and Magog as the number-four sign on the list.

According to Islamic teaching, Gog and Magog are two groups of Turks that were spreading corruption through the earth during the time of Abraham. Finally, to keep them in check, they were enclosed behind a great barrier. Though they have tried in vain for centuries to climb over or dig under the wall, they will not be able to do so until Allah decrees their release. Then the barrier will collapse, and Gog and Magog will pour out in all directions, rushing into the land of Israel to attack the Muslims there. When Jesus (according to Muslim teaching) prays against Gog and Magog, Allah will wipe them out by means of some kind of disease or plague.[6] The disease is described as either infectious, lethal boils, or a disease that eats the flesh from their bones.

Does that sound a bit familiar? It should. Mohammed clearly "borrowed" that imagery straight from Ezekiel 38—with a few convenient changes to fit his own ends. Ezekiel 38:22 specifically says that God will judge the invaders with disease and with blood. What's so interesting to me is that although Muslims believe in the prophecy of Gog and Magog, they appear to be totally ignorant of the fact that the nations mentioned in the prophecy that will be destroyed by God are all Muslim nations today, with the exception of Russia. One of their ten great signs of the end will actually be fulfilled by them when they attack Israel in the last days. Gog and Magog are a vast group of Muslim nations.

But I don't want you to just take my word for it. Let's continue to answer that *who* question. Who are some of the other nations who will join this invading army?

THREE

TRACKING THE BEAR

The next nation on Ezekiel's list is Rosh. For many years students of Bible prophecy have noticed the obvious similarity between the words Rosh and Russia. As you can imagine, the view that Rosh is Russia gained great popularity in the decades following World War II when Russia and the Soviet Union emerged as a world power opposed to Israel and the West.

We have to be careful, however, not to make identifications based upon the similarity of the sound of words. Before we jump to any conclusions, let's see if Rosh really could be Russia.

IS "ROSH" RUSSIA?

The name *Rosh* is found in Ezekiel 38:2 and again in 39:1. The word *rosh* in Hebrew simply means "head, top, summit, or chief." It is a very common word and is common to all Semitic languages. It occurs approximately 750 times in the Old Testament, including its root and derivatives.

The problem is that the word *rosh* in Ezekiel can be translated as either a proper noun or an adjective. Many translations take *rosh* as an adjective and translate it as the word *chief* or something equivalent. The King James Version, the Revised Standard Version, the New American Bible, the New Living Translation, and the New International Version all adopt this translation.

I believe the better translation is to take *rosh* as a proper noun referring to a specific place. This is the translation adopted in the Jerusalem Bible, the New English Bible, and the New American Standard Bible. The great Hebrew scholars C. F. Keil and Wilhelm Gesenius both state clearly that *rosh* in Ezekiel 38:2–3 and 39:1 is the name of a geographical location.[7]

Also, the Septuagint, the Greek translation of the Old Testament, translates *rosh* as the proper name *Ros*.

This is especially significant since the Septuagint was translated only three centuries after Ezekiel was written. An ancient group of people known as the Sarmatians were known as the Ras, Rashu, and Rus who inhabited the land of Rasapu. These people inhabited the area that today we know as southern Russia.

Gesenius confidently says that *Rosh* in Ezekiel 38–39 is "undoubtedly the Russians, who are mentioned by the Byzantine writers of the tenth century under the name *Ros,* dwelling to the north of Taurus…as dwelling on the river Rha (Wolga)."[8]

ROSH TODAY

Many people might be surprised to learn that one of the key places mentioned in Bible prophecy is Russia. Scripture predicts that the great Russian bear will rise in the last days to mount a furious invasion of Israel. Ezekiel predicted that in the latter times Israel would be invaded by a people "from remote parts of the north" (38:6, 15). The nation that is most distantly north from Israel is Russia.

On December 25, 1979, the Soviets invaded

Afghanistan. The Russian war in Afghanistan had been called by many "the great bear trap." When Russian troops withdrew from Afghanistan in 1989, the mighty empire had suffered its greatest humiliation. For many, that event marked the end of the cold war.

Two years later, when the Soviet Union was dissolved in December 1991, many believed that the bear had gone into permanent hibernation. But the Russian bear today is in some ways a much more dangerous bear than ever before. Her economy in shambles, she is a *hungry* bear. Although the Russian economy has improved since the economic meltdown in 1998, there are still some alarming numbers to ponder:

- 2 percent population drop since 1992 due to deteriorating health and skyrocketing numbers of AIDS cases,
- 40 percent of population below poverty level,
- 10 percent unemployment, and
- 20 percent inflation.[9]

Russia is not only a hungry bear; she is also a humiliated bear. With her great Soviet Union dissolved, she is a mother bear robbed of her cubs. As a result, she is desperately seeking to re-exert her influence, especially in the five former Soviet republics in Central Asia…and also in the Middle East.

Russia is alive and well today. In what has been dubbed "The Great Game," she competes vigorously with the U.S. and China for influence in and access to Central Asian policy and resources. Russia announced in January 2001 that it would join Kazakhstan, Kyrgyzstan, and Tajikistan to create a rapid-deployment force of three thousand men based in Tajikistan.[10] Russia has also continued to develop close ties to Iran. We will look at this developing relationship more in chapter 5.

The fulfillment of God's prophecies concerning Russia seem closer than ever before. As we track the bear in the end times, we discover that her footprints lead right to the land of Israel.

The Russians are coming! They are coming in the future to invade the land of Israel. But they won't be alone. They will be joined by a vast Islamic alliance of nations.

THE UNLIKELY ALLY

I'm a native Oklahoman—a born-and-raised Okie. And I love my home state. But I have to admit that we have some towns here with some pretty strange names. A few that come to mind include Gotebo (pronounced Go-tee-bow), Bowlegs, Oologah, Tishomingo, Pocasset, and, of course, my personal favorite: Hitchcock.

But when it comes to difficult names for places, Oklahoma has nothing on the Bible. The Bible is filled with ancient names that are very strange to us today. Ezekiel 38 is no exception. We have already looked at three of these strange names (Gog, Magog, and Rosh), identified them, and shown how they fit into the prophetic scenario of Scripture.

Ezekiel 38:2 and 38:6 list four more ancient names that we need to identify to understand this great prophecy: Meshech, Tubal, Gomer, and Beth-togarmah. Interestingly, all four of these names point us to the same location. Let's look at each of these names and discover another ally in the end-time coalition against Israel.

MESHECH AND TUBAL

Meshech and Tubal are mentioned together in Ezekiel 38:2. Meshech and Tubal were the sixth and fifth sons of Japheth, the son of Noah (see Genesis 10:2). The generally accepted view of most prophecy students for many years was that they refer to the cities of Moscow and Tobolsk in Russia. These identifications were popularized by the notes on Ezekiel 38:2 in *The Scofield Study Bible.* "That the primary reference is to the Northern (European) powers headed by Russia, all agree.... The reference to Meshech and Tubal (Moscow and Tobolsk) is a clear mark of identification."[11]

C. I. Scofield's view seems to have been primarily

based on the similarity of sound in these names and their close proximity to Rosh, which probably is Russia. Meshech and Tubal are mentioned together in Ezekiel 27:13 as trading partners with ancient Tyre (modern Lebanon). It is highly doubtful that ancient Tyre was trading with people in the area as far north as Moscow and Tobolsk.

A closer study of these names reveals that Meshech and Tubal are the ancient Moschi/Mushki and Tubalu/Tibareni peoples who dwelled in the area around, primarily south of, the Black and Caspian Seas in Ezekiel's day. These nations today are in the modern country of Turkey, possibly parts of southern Russia, and northern Iran.[12]

GOMER

God identifies another participant in the end-time confederation of nations as ancient Gomer, who was the first son of Japheth, the son of Noah (see Genesis 10:2–3). When I was growing up, I always heard prophecy teachers identify Gomer in Ezekiel 38 as Germany, or more specifically East Germany, since Gomer and Germany sound somewhat alike. That association also fit nicely with the world political situation at that time, East Germany being a part of the Warsaw Pact and Soviet empire.

A closer examination, however, reveals that the Gomerites were the ancient Cimmerians, expelled in 700 B.C. from the southern steppes of Russia into the area we know today as Turkey.

BETH-TOGARMAH

According to Genesis 10:3, Togarmah was the third son of Gomer. The word *Beth* at the beginning of the word is the Hebrew word for "house" or "place of." It simply means "house or place of Togarmah." The only indication about Togarmah's location in the Bible is found in Ezekiel 38:6: "Beth-togarmah from the remote parts of the north with all its troops." Therefore, we know that Togarmah is from the far north of Israel.

Going back to Ezekiel's time, we discover that there was a city in Cappodocia (modern Turkey) known as Tegarma, Tagarma, Til-garimmu, and Takarama. This fits Ezekiel's identification exactly because Turkey is far north of Israel.

LET'S TALK TURKEY

It's interesting to me that four of the ancient locations Ezekiel gives are found today in the nation of Turkey. Clearly, God seems to be emphasizing Turkey's part in the end-time coalition.

Turkey today is not as hard-core Muslim as some of the other nations in Ezekiel's list, but they are an Islamic nation. And according to God's Word they will be a part of this end-time coalition. What do we know about Turkey today?

In recent years, Turkey has experienced a rash of terrorist attacks by Islamic radicals. There has also been a recent rise of political Islam. Necmettin Erbakan has led pro-Islamic political parties from "the political wilderness in the 1960s to become Turkey's biggest and best-disciplined [parties] in the 1990s."[13] In municipal elections on March 27, 1994, a group called the Association for a New World Outlook in Europe (AMGT)—a branch of the Turkish Welfare Party (RP)—won 19 percent of the votes in local elections. In their platform, they advocate the nonviolent (thus far) establishment of a Turkish Islamic republic, opposition to Israel, and the worldwide spread and rule of Islam. The Welfare Party won 327 mayoralties, including those of 28 cities.[14] The AMGT boasts 400 branches throughout the European area of Turkey and claims 30,000 members.[15]

We also know that Turkey has gone to great lengths to gain inroads into Central Asia (Magog) since the breakup of the Soviet Union. Since Turkey is linked to Central Asia both ethnically and linguistically, it has a natural relationship to these nations. This is just another example of the alliances being forged between the nations listed in Ezekiel 38.

Turkey is the only nation in the world with land on two continents: Europe and Asia. The nation's geography is a mirror of its political and military position as well. It is being pulled both ways. Turkey covets recognition by the West—even to the point of desiring inclusion in the European Union. Turkey regularly cooperates with the United States in military operations in the region. At this writing, her soldiers are engaged in peacekeeping duties in war-shattered Afghanistan.

But never forget that Turkey is still a Muslim nation.

The Turkish government pays the salaries of 60,000 imams and dictates the contents of their weekly sermons, often down to the last word.[16]

As Nicole and Hugh Pope observe, "Islam is the most controversial issue to divide the Turkish republic since it was founded in 1923."[17] We don't know all the details of what will happen in Turkey to cause them to join Gog's coalition. But whatever twists and turns may occur in the days and years ahead, Turkey will join the end-time Islamic coalition and its disastrous invasion of the land of Israel.

SEVEN DOWN, THREE TO GO

Let's pause for a moment to review what we've seen so far in seven of the names on Ezekiel's top-ten list of nations. We have discovered that a man known only as Gog will lead Russia, the nations of Central Asia, and Turkey in an end-time alliance that comes against Israel.

That alone should be enough to grab our attention.

But wait until you see the identity of the next three nations!

FIVE

THE ISLAMIC LEGION

In his January 2002 State of the Union address, President George W. Bush made a brief statement that created quite a controversy. What was this debated comment? He named the nations of Iraq, Iran, and North Korea as forming "the axis of evil" in our world today.

Many today seem to object to any notion of evil. In Ezekiel 38:10, however, God says that the end-time invaders of Israel have an "evil plan."

God doesn't hesitate at all to use the word *evil*.

Just as President Bush had his list of three nations he identified as the axis of evil, in Ezekiel 38:5, God lists three nations that we might call "the end-time axis of evil." The text speaks of *"Persia, Ethiopia* and *Put* with them, all of them with shield and helmet." Interestingly, one of the nations on God's list is also on the president's list.

These final three names on "God's Top-Ten Most Wanted List" are part of the Islamic legion that will meet its doom in Israel in the end times. Let's look at these final three names in Ezekiel 38:1–7 to fill in the complete picture of the end-time Islamic alliance.

PLACING PERSIA

Ezekiel 38:5 lists Persia as another nation that will join the end-time alliance against Israel. This is probably the easiest of the nations in Ezekiel 38 to place. Ezekiel wrote his prophecy in about 580 B.C., while Babylon was still the ruling empire. At that time, Persia was not a dominating power, although Persians did sell themselves as mercenaries to other nations (see Ezekiel 27:10). But about forty years later, in 539 B.C., the Persians conquered the mighty city of Babylon.

To discover where Persia is today, all you have to do is look at an ancient map of the Persian empire. Where was it centered?

In the land we know today as Iran.

In fact, the name *Persia* was changed to *Iran* in foreign usage in March 1935 and then to the Islamic Republic of Iran in 1979 during the Iranian Revolution.

According to God's Word, therefore, the Iranians will join with Turkey, the nations of Central Asia, and Russia to invade Israel in the end times. By the way, Iran is the nation included in President Bush's "axis of evil." I hardly have to say much to convince anyone today that Iran is an archenemy of Israel and the West. But you may not realize how Iran is related to some of the other nations listed in Ezekiel 38.

Between 1989 and 1993, Iran spent $10 billion to purchase weapons from Russia and also began to buy Russian nuclear and ballistic-missile technology. Iran currently has two nuclear-reactor sites. In 1992, Iran signed an agreement with Russia to revitalize their nuclear reactors that had been damaged in the war with Iraq. The agreement called for Russia to supply Iran with two 440-megawatt reactors. It is estimated that Iran will be able to assemble nuclear weapons in five to seven years.[18]

In March 2001, Iran's President Mohammad Khatami visited Russia to forge stronger ties between the two nations. After the meeting, Russian president Vladimir Putin said that Russia would resume sales of conventional arms to Iran, and help Iran complete its nuclear reactor near Bushehr.

The Tehran Conference in Iran in 1991 was attended by members of radical Islamic movements and terrorist groups from at least forty countries. At this conference the attendees declared themselves to be against making any kind of peace with Israel.[19]

Iran is also a key supporter of Hizbullah, the Party of God, which terrorizes Israel on a regular basis. You might also remember the huge shipment of Iranian arms headed to the Palestinians that was seized in the Red Sea by the Israelis in early 2002.

Since the September 11 terrorist attack on New York and Washington, D.C., Iran has taken center stage to bring Muslim and Arab nations together against Israel—and the United States. Syed Shahzad notes,

The Iranian initiative seeks to persuade some of those countries that initially sided with the U.S.

into switching camps…. And these developments have brought many Arab and Middle Eastern nations closer together. Sources said that Iran played an important role in this and had been pursuing countries such as Saudi Arabia and Kuwait in particular to help them restore their relations with Iraq so that all Muslim nations can devise a common strategy against Israel in the Middle East…. The test now will be how fast Arab and Muslim nations move to form a common stance and how quickly the U.S. takes measures to counter them.[20]

There is much more that we could say about Iran, but make no mistake. When Gog rallies his last-days assault force, the Iranians will be one of the first to sign up.

THE KINGDOM OF CUSH

There are two North African nations mentioned in Ezekiel's list. The first is Ethiopia, or (more correctly translated) Cush. The ancient kingdom of Cush in Ezekiel's day was the land just south of Egypt on the

Nile River. Today the nation that occupies this land is Sudan. One would be hard-pressed to find a more rabid enemy of Israel and the West today than Sudan.

On June 30, 1989, General Omar Hassan al-Bashir mounted a successful military coup d'état in Sudan. However, the real power behind the new regime was Hassan al-Turabi and his extremist party, the National Islamic Front (NIF). Sudan was immediately and totally converted into an Islamic military dictatorship.

Sudan supported Iraq during the Gulf War, gave refuge to Osama bin Laden from 1991 to 1996 and became a rallying place for every hard-line Islamic movement imaginable. In April 1991, in the wake of the Gulf War, al-Turabi along with leaders from about fifty hard-line Islamic movements from the Arab Middle East, Iran, Afghanistan, and Pakistan—including Palestinian leader Yasser Arafat—founded the Popular Arab and Islamic Conference (PAIC). His intent was to crystallize all the hard-line Islamic militants and nationalists under a single banner. This gathering was followed by similar meetings in December 1993 and March–April 1995.[21] Some have called

Sudan "terrorism's new Mecca." Madeleine Albright has called Sudan "a viper's nest of terrorism."

One of the most amazing things about Ezekiel 38 is that God placed Persia and Cush right next to each other approximately 2,600 years ago as end-time allies against Israel (see v. 5). This is incredible because contemporary Iran and Sudan have a very close relationship. We could call it the "Iran-Sudan connection." Sudan is Iran's best ally. Iran supplies Sudan with military supplies, oil, and military training, and Sudan gives Iran docking rights at Port Sudan on Red Sea shipping routes. This connection is here right before our eyes, setting the stage for what God predicted over two and a half millennia ago!

WHERE DO WE PUT PUT?

The next nation after Sudan in Ezekiel's list is Put, or as some versions correctly translate it, Libya (see Ezekiel 38:5, NLT). Ancient Put was the land just to the west of Egypt.[22]

Libya's current leader, Muammar Qaddafi, took control in 1969. Ever since that time, Libya has been an international rogue state and sponsor of international terror. While some other Muslim nations offer at least token efforts toward resolving the Middle East crisis, Libya refuses to recognize Israel's right to even exist.

When the call for the final jihad comes, Libya will willingly fall in line.

MANY PEOPLES WITH YOU

We have now finished identifying the specific names on "God's Top-Ten List" in Ezekiel 38:1–7, but this list may not be exhaustive. The last four words in Ezekiel 38:6, "many peoples with you," give us a clue that more nations may be allied with this coalition than the specific ones listed.

When you look at a map of the specific nations that Ezekiel lists, you will notice that they are all somewhat distant from Israel. By mentioning these distant enemies and then concluding with the words "many peoples with you," God may be letting us know that many more near enemies of Israel will join this coalition of invaders.

Who could some of these near enemies or "many peoples" be? Perhaps other Islamic nations such as Iraq, Syria, Jordan, and Egypt.

CHARTING THE END TIMES

Here is a chart that brings together all the nations in
Ezekiel's list of Israel's last-days enemies.

ANCIENT NAME	MODERN NATION	EXPLANATION
Rosh	Russia	Ancient Sarmatians—known as Rashu, Rasapu, Ros, and Rus.
Magog	Central Asia	Ancient Scythians—Islamic southern republics of the former Soviet Union with a population of 60 million Muslims. This territory could include modern Afghanistan.
Meshech	Turkey	Ancient Muschki and Musku in Cilicia and Cappadocia.
Tubal	Turkey (also southern Russia and Iran)	Ancient Tubalu in Cappadocia.
Persia	Iran	Name changed from Persia to Iran in 1935.
Ethiopia	Sudan	Ancient Cush, south of Egypt.
Put	Libya	Ancient Put, west of Egypt.
Gomer	Turkey	Ancient Cimmerians—from the seventh century to first century B.C. in central/western Anatolia.
Beth-togarmah	Turkey	Til-garimmu—between ancient Carchemish and Haran (southern Turkey).
Many peoples with you	Other Islamic nations	Possibly Iraq, Syria, Jordan, and Egypt.

From this list it is clear that at least six key allies (and possibly others) will come together for this end-time invasion of Israel: Russia, Turkey, Iran, Libya, Sudan, and the nations of Central Asia. Amazingly, all of these nations except Russia are Muslim nations. Iran, Libya, and Sudan, three of Israel's most ardent opponents, are also listed by the U.S. government as states that support terrorism. Many of these nations are either forming or strengthening their ties as these words are being written.

This list of nations reads like the headlines of this week's newspaper. It's not too difficult to imagine these nations conspiring to invade Israel in the near future. And according to God's Word, that is exactly what they will do.

It could be *very* soon.

HOW CLOSE ARE WE?

H ow much longer, Daddy?"
"Are we there yet, Mommy?"
"When are we gonna get there?"

Every parent has experienced those questions from the backseat. It might be on a long family vacation, or just across town to Grandpa and Grandma's house.

Kids don't like to wait. They want to know "How much longer until my birthday?" "How much longer until Christmas?" "How much longer till my friends come over?"

If we know Jesus Christ, we are God's children, and we too ask such questions—especially in the area of

Bible prophecy. Whenever I travel to speak about prophecy or give an interview, I always hear the questions: When? How much longer? When will the Rapture take place? When will the temple be rebuilt in Jerusalem? How long until Babylon will be rebuilt? When?

Even Jesus' disciples asked Him, "When?" on several occasions (see Matthew 24:1–3; Acts 1:6–7).

Most of the time when I'm asked the *when* question, I have to say that we simply don't know. But sometimes our loving Father does tell His questioning children when certain events will occur. I don't mean that He circles a date in red on the calendar, giving the exact day or year, but He speaks in general terms that we can understand.

After identifying the nations that will invade Israel in the end times, Ezekiel addresses the *when* question. When will this invasion take place? The prophet provides three important clues that help us narrow down the time of this invasion. All three clues can be found in one verse: Ezekiel 38:8.

"After many days you will be summoned; in the latter years you will come into the land that is restored from the sword, whose inhabitants have been gathered from many nations to the mountains of Israel which had been a continual waste; but its people were brought out from the nations, and they are living securely, all of them."

Let's examine these three clues and see how close we may be to the time of this invasion.

TIMING CLUE #1

It must be the "latter years" or "last days" when this invasion occurs.

The first clue regarding the chronology of this event is found in the phrases "After many days" and "in the latter years." According to God, this invasion will occur "in the latter years." Another similar phrase occurs later in this chapter in Ezekiel 38:16. "It shall come about in *the last days* that I will bring you against My land" (emphasis added).

Ezekiel 38:8 is the only occurrence of the Hebrew phrase "in the latter years" in the Old Testament. However the Hebrew phrase "in the last days" (or latter days) that is found in Ezekiel 38:16 occurs a total of fourteen times in the Old Testament. This phrase is normally used in reference to Israel's final time of distress or to Israel's final restoration to the Messianic kingdom (see Isaiah 2:2; Jeremiah 23:20; 30:24; Hosea 3:5; Micah 4:1).

The second use of the phrase "latter days" or "last days" in the Old Testament is in Deuteronomy 4:30 where it describes both the future time of tribulation for Israel as well as her ultimate restoration and blessing. "When you are in distress and all these things have come upon you, in the latter days you will return to the LORD your God and listen to His voice." These timing phrases in Ezekiel 38 clearly eliminate any past fulfillment for this invasion and reveal that it's still to come in the future.[23]

The timing of the Battle of Gog and Magog during the "latter years" or "last days" also tells us that it will occur after the rapture of the church to heaven. Since this invasion will occur in the last days, which is the time of Israel's future tribulation and restoration, and since the Rapture occurs before the Tribulation begins, then this indicates that the Battle of Gog and

Magog will occur after the rapture of all believers in Christ to heaven.

TIMING CLUE #2

Israel must be regathered to her land when this invasion occurs.

The second clue in Ezekiel 38:8 is found in the words "whose inhabitants have been gathered from many nations to the mountains of Israel."

God is telling these invading nations that sometime in the future they will attack Israel when she has been restored to her land in the latter years or last days. This can only be referring to the regathering of Israel that began in 1948 when many Jews returned to their homeland for the first time in nineteen centuries. This point is further supported by the fact that Ezekiel 36–37, the two chapters that immediately precede Ezekiel 38–39, focus on the regathering of Israel to her land in the last days. God is telling us clearly that sometime *after* this regathering begins is when this invasion will occur.[24] Since this regathering has begun and continues today, this part of the end-time stage furniture is already in place.

TIMING CLUE #3

Israel must be at rest when this invasion occurs.

Ezekiel adds a third important detail to narrow down the time of this invasion. He tells us that Israel must not only be regathered to her land for this invasion to occur, but also be *at rest* when this invasion takes place. This point is emphasized three times in Ezekiel 38.

> "But its people were brought out from the nations, and they are living securely, all of them." (38:8)

> 'Those who are at rest, that live securely, all of them living without walls, and having no bars or gates.' (38:11)

> 'Thus says the Lord GOD, "On that day when My people Israel are living securely, will you not know it?"' (38:14)

Since 1948, Israel has *never* enjoyed a time of peace and safety when she could let her guard down.

Modern Israel has never really had a time of peace—only brief respites without full-fledged war. Looking at the situation in the Middle East today, we might legitimately ask, "When will Israel ever enjoy a time of rest and security like the one described in Ezekiel 38?"

There are only two times in Israel's future when the Bible indicates that she will be at peace. The first is a brief three-and-a-half-year period of peace during the first half of the seven-year Tribulation, which will begin when the Antichrist makes a covenant or peace treaty with Israel (see Daniel 9:27).

The second time of peace for Israel will be when the Prince of Peace, the Lord Jesus, returns to earth from heaven to destroy Israel's enemies and inaugurate his one-thousand-year kingdom of peace and joy centered in Israel (see Revelation 19:11–20:10). However, Isaiah 2:4 says explicitly that this time will be a time when there will be no war.

> And He will judge between the nations, and will render decisions for many peoples; and they will hammer their swords into plowshares and their spears into pruning hooks. Nation

will not lift up sword against nation, and never again will they learn war.

TIME IS OF THE ESSENCE

Putting all these clues together, the only time period in the future that fits the scenario described in Ezekiel 38 is the first half of the tribulation period after the church has been raptured to heaven and when Israel is living under the peace and protection of her covenant with Antichrist.[25]

The Hebrew word *betah* (securely) is used three times in Ezekiel 38 (see vv. 8, 11, 14). Interestingly, this word "expresses that sense of well-being and security which results from having something or someone in whom to place confidence."[26] This is the exact situation that Israel will find herself in when she enters into her covenant with Antichrist.

As the eminent prophecy scholar John Walvoord writes,

> Under that covenant, Israel will be able to relax, for their Gentile enemies will have

become their friends, apparently guaranteed their borders and promised them freedom. During that first three and one-half years, we have the one time when regathered Israel is at rest and secure. Apparently, Russia will invade the land of Israel during that period, possibly toward its close, and the Scriptures will then be fulfilled.[27]

I agree with Dr. Walvoord that this invasion will occur near the close of the first half of the Tribulation.[28] This means that the Battle of Gog and Magog will occur at least three and a half years before the War of Armageddon, or World War III, at the end of the Tribulation. The Battle of Gog and Magog will probably be the first great war of the tribulation period.

How soon will this happen?

There is no way to say for sure. But we *can* say that the stage is set. Israel is in the process of being regathered. Within the next few years it is estimated that over half of the Jews worldwide will be back in the land of Israel. The regathering is literally happening before our eyes.

But what about that time of rest? Could it be near?

Well, let's think about it in these terms. What's the one problem in the world that everyone wants to see solved? The chronic Middle East chaos. And who is beginning to step in more and more as a mediator in the peace talks?

Europe.

The foreign minister of the European Union has been a key player in the recent rounds of Middle East peace talks. This is exactly the scenario predicted in the Bible. God's Word says that Antichrist will arise from Europe, the reunited Roman empire, and will bring peace, albeit temporarily, to Israel.

THE RIDER ON THE RED HORSE

Revelation 6–19 is the most detailed picture of the coming seven-year tribulation period. These fourteen chapters are the heart of the book of Revelation. Revelation 6:1–8 record the opening of the seal judgments that inaugurate this seven-year period of hell on earth. The first four of these seals are often called the four horsemen of the Apocalypse: a rider on a white horse, a rider on a red horse, a rider on a black horse, and a rider on a pale horse.

The first two of these horsemen parallel what we see in Ezekiel 38. First, the rider on the white horse pictures the emergence of Antichrist on the world scene. Revelation 6:1–2 says,

> Then I saw when the Lamb broke one of the seven seals, and I heard one of the four living creatures saying as with a voice of thunder, "Come." I looked, and behold, a white horse, and he who sat on it had a bow; and a crown was given to him, and he went out conquering and to conquer.

Notice that the Antichrist rides a white horse to imitate the true Christ (see Revelation 19:11) and that he carries a bow—but no arrows. This suggests that at first his conquest will be a bloodless one. He will threaten war but achieve his victory through peace. He will conceal his iron fist in the velvet glove of peace.

Second, the rider on the red horse pictures the brutal, bloody slaughter of war. The word for *red* in the original Greek is *pyrros* (fiery red). He rides forth with a great sword to take the peace from the earth that was ushered in by the Antichrist. Revelation 6:3–4 says,

> When He broke the second seal, I heard the second living creature saying, "Come." And another, a red horse, went out; and to him who sat on it, it was granted to take peace from the earth, and that men would slay one another; and a great sword was given to him.

I believe the red horse pictures a general state of warfare that begins to break out all over the world in the first half of the Tribulation—just as Jesus predicted in Matthew 24:6–7—and continues until Armageddon. But more specifically, I believe that the rider on the red horse symbolizes the first great bloodbath of the tribulation period—the Battle of Gog and Magog. This battle is the harbinger of what's ahead for planet earth in the Tribulation.

This is another reason why I believe the Battle of Gog and Magog will happen during the first half of the Tribulation. It fits precisely with the timing of the rider on the red horse in Revelation 6:3–4.

APPROACHING HOOFBEATS

Writing twenty years ago in his powerful book *Approaching Hoofbeats,* Billy Graham looked out on the horizon and saw the red horse of hot war galloping forth.

> Listen! The distant sounds of those same hoofbeats can be heard closing in…. It is completely naive and insane for us to ignore the fact that the ominous rider who brings war is, even now, riding recklessly in our direction. Our earth has shrunk into a global village; we are all neighbors. The foreboding sound of the hoofbeats of the red horse pulses like an erratic heartbeat at the center of our beleaguered planet.[29]

As I look around, I couldn't agree more with Billy Graham. With the continual cry for peace in the Middle East and the rise of militant Islam, it seems that the rider on the red horse could be mounting up. It's not too difficult to envision these events unfolding very soon.

How close are we? We could be very close!

The house lights appear to be dimming. The curtain could go up at any moment. The Rapture could occur today, before you finish reading this page. And then the Antichrist will come on the scene to make his peace with Israel. The sands in the prophetic hourglass will begin to empty.

SEVEN

THE FINAL JIHAD

L ike most Americans, up until a few years ago I had never even heard the word *jihad*. Now it's a common word in our national vocabulary.

Jihad, the traditional Muslim word for holy war against the unfaithful, is ingrained into our national psyche. I went to a large bookstore in Oklahoma City recently and was staggered to see an entire section of books about Osama bin Laden, al-Qaida, militant Islam, and the Koran. But the most common word in the book titles was the explosive word *jihad. Jihad* is everywhere today, and I don't believe it's an accident. It all fits into God's script for the end times.

I believe that Ezekiel 38–39 describes the final

jihad. Notice the reasons God gives for *why* this horde of nations invades Israel.

> "You will go up, you will come like a storm; you will be like a cloud covering the land, you and all your troops, and many peoples with you." 'Thus says the Lord GOD, "It will come about on that day, that thoughts will come into your mind and you will devise an evil plan, and you will say, 'I will go up against the land of unwalled villages. I will go against those who are at rest, that live securely, all of them living without walls and having no bars or gates, to capture spoil and to seize plunder, to turn your hand against the waste places which are now inhabited, and against the people who are gathered from the nations, who have acquired cattle and goods, who live at the center of the world.' . . . 'Have you come to capture spoil? Have you assembled your company to seize plunder, to carry away silver and gold, to take away cattle and goods, to capture great spoil?'" (Ezekiel 38:9–12, 13b)

Although Ezekiel never uses the word *jihad,* he does give us three reasons why these nations invade Israel, and the reasons they attack seem to describe what we know today as jihad. See if you agree.

DEATH TO ISRAEL

According to God, the first reason these nations come is to cover the land of Israel like a storm, to turn their hand against Israel. They will be motivated by a Satanic hatred for the Jewish people to completely cover their land and wipe them off the face of the earth.

Of course, this is nothing new today. This is the stated goal of almost every Islamic nation. Since 1948, the Muslim nations of the world have been in a constant state of war with Israel. The only Arab/Muslim nations not in a declared state of war with Israel today are Egypt, Turkey, and Jordan, yet even they would be glad to see Israel eliminated.

PLUNDER!

The second reason these nations will come is to cash in on the wealth of Israel. God says they come "to capture spoil and to seize plunder…to capture great spoil." Simply stated, these nations will come out of greed, envy, and jealousy to take all they can from Israel. They want not only to eradicate Israel, but to enrich themselves at her expense.

DOWN WITH THE WEST

The third and final reason they will attack is to come against the Antichrist and the Western World. Remember that when this invasion occurs, Israel will be enjoying the security of her peace treaty with the Antichrist (see Daniel 9:27). The invaders will come upon "those who are at rest, that live securely, all of them living without walls and having no bars or gates" (38:11). Since Israel will be under western protection, an attack against Israel will also be an attack against her western allies, primarily the Antichrist and his European Union…and possibly the United States.

Again, this is exactly what we see today. Militant Islamic regimes would love nothing more than to invade Israel at a time of supposed peace and tranquillity, crush her, and plunder her of all her wealth. Their venomous hatred for Israel knows no bounds. And if they could also bring a blow against the West at the same time…well, that would just be icing on the cake.

FINAL JIHAD, FINAL JUDGMENT

This invasion will indeed be jihad all right, but it will also be the final jihad. It will be the last great attempt by militant Islamic countries to wipe out the Jewish people and their promised land once and for all.

The next question that immediately comes to mind is, How will it end? What will happen when these nations invade Israel? Who will win?

What will happen when Gog meets God?

EIGHT

THE "ONE-DAY WAR"

I'll never forget the first time I went to Israel, back in June 1994. The sights, sounds, and smells were unforgettable.

I got to see Mount Carmel where Elijah faced the prophets of Baal. I visited Megiddo, Nazareth, the Sea of Galilee, Capernaum, Jericho, Jerusalem, and a hundred other thrilling sites. But there was one area we visited that deeply affected me, one that I didn't know much about before the trip.

It's the area known today as the Golan Heights.

As we traveled in this area, we saw abandoned Syrian bunkers and burned-out Israeli tanks and personnel carriers—the leftovers of the Six-Day War from June 5 to June 10, 1967. Our guide told stirring stories of the heroics of Israeli troops when Israel was invaded by troops from Syria, Iraq, Jordan, Egypt, and Saudi Arabia. As a result of that war, Israel captured the Golan Heights, the West Bank (including East Jerusalem), the Gaza Strip, the Sinai, and the temple mount.

It was the greatest hour in modern Israeli history.

Israel had repelled an all-out Arab attack and won decisively.

Someday in the future, the events of the Six-Day War will be repeated—with a few crucial differences. As Yogi Berra would say, it will look like "déjà vu all over again." When Gog and his allies invade Israel in the last days, it will look like Israel has finally met her doom. She will be surrounded on all sides: Russia and Turkey from the north, Iran from the east, Libya from the west, Sudan from the south, and possibly many of the nations in between from every direction. Israel will be caught in an inescapable pincer move. Let's look at what will happen when this invasion occurs.

DIPLOMATIC PROTEST

The first thing that happens as this invasion develops is that a small group of countries lodge a lame protest against these invaders. That sounds strikingly similar to something that would happen in modern international diplomacy, doesn't it?

Ezekiel 38:13 says,

> "Sheba and Dedan and the merchants of Tarshish with all its villages will say to you, 'Have you come to capture spoil? Have you assembled your company to seize plunder, to carry away silver and gold, to take away cattle and goods, to capture great spoil?'"

The specific nations who question Gog's actions are identified as "Sheba and Dedan and the merchants of Tarshish." Sheba and Dedan are not difficult to identify. Sheba and Dedan were ancient names for the land we know today as Saudi Arabia.

Tarshish, on the other hand, is not so simple to identify. However, the weight of authority is that Tarshish is ancient Tartessus in the present-day nation of Spain. This view is supported by both Brown-Driver-Briggs and the Hebrew scholar Gesenius.[30]

Tarshish was a wealthy, flourishing colony of the Phoenicians located in modern Spain, which exported silver, iron, tin and lead (see Jeremiah 10:9; Ezekiel 27:12, 25). But note that Ezekiel refers not just to Tarshish, but to "the merchants of Tarshish with all its villages" (NASB) or "the merchants of Tarshish and all her villages" (NIV). The better translation is probably "Tarshish, with all the young lions" (KJV). The New International Version cites "her strong lions" as an alternate reading.

Young lions are often used in Scripture to refer to energetic rulers. Therefore, the young lions who act with Tarshish to verbally oppose Gog's invasion are strong military and political leaders who act in concert with Tarshish.

Where was Tarshish in Ezekiel's day? It was in the farthest west regions of the known world, in Spain. When God commanded Jonah to go preach to Nineveh (about 500 miles northeast of Israel), Jonah headed to Tarshish, or Spain, which was as far in the other direction as he could go (see Jonah 1:1–3).

As we know, Spain is in modern Europe, more specifically western Europe. Tarshish, or modern Spain, could be used by Ezekiel to represent the nations of western Europe that will join Saudi Arabia in denouncing this invasion.

Tarshish is associated in Scripture with the West. "The western kings of Tarshish and the islands will bring him tribute" (Psalm 72:10, NLT). The young lions of Tarshish could be a reference to the colonies that emerged from Europe—including the United States. If this is true, then the young lions of Tarshish describes the United States in the last days joining in with her European and Saudi allies to lodge a formal protest against the Russian-Islamic aggressors.

Whether you take these young lions to refer to the United States or just as a reference to the western powers of the last days, the scenario that is developed in Ezekiel 38 fits the present world political situation precisely. Russia continues to build alliances with Middle Eastern nations. Sudan (Cush) and Iran (Persia) are strong allies. The Muslim nations of Central Asia (Magog) have developing ties with Iran, Russia, and Turkey. The hatred for Israel by the

Middle Eastern Muslim nations continues to boil. It is not too difficult to imagine the nations mentioned in Ezekiel 38:1–7 coming together under Russian leadership to mount a furious attack against Israel.

But what is the one Middle Eastern nation that constantly sides with the West against the radical Islamic elements in that region of the world? The obvious answer is Saudi Arabia—ancient Sheba and Dedan. The U.S. and NATO use bases in Saudi Arabia to launch strikes against Iraq and to monitor the entire Persian Gulf area.

The exact alignment of nations predicted in Ezekiel 38 was clearly evidenced in the Gulf War in the early 1990s and continues for the most part today. The United States, Western Europe, and Saudi Arabia were allied against Iraq while Russia, Iran, Sudan, Libya, and most of the other nations of the Middle East and Persian Gulf were aligned with Iraq, or at least against the West.

GOG VERSUS GOD

Gog and his allies will totally disregard these diplomatic protests against the invasion of Israel. They are bent on war and destruction. It's the perfect time, and they will not back down. When these nations invade the land of Israel, it will look like the biggest mismatch in history. It will make the invasions of Israel by Arab nations in 1967 and 1973 pale in comparison.

When Gog assembles this last-days strike force, it will look like Israel is finished. Israel will be completely surrounded. This time the Jewish people will not be able to overcome their enemies by their own strength and ingenuity. Israel will be totally overwhelmed. Gog and his army will cover Israel like a cloud. And yet the Bible says that God will come to the rescue for His people. Almighty God will intervene to win the battle for His people. Ezekiel 38–39 describes what we might call the "One-Day War"—or even the "One-Hour War"—because God will quickly and completely annihilate the Islamic invaders from the face of the earth by supernatural means.

Here is how Ezekiel graphically describes it:

"It will come about on that day, when Gog comes against the land of Israel," declares the Lord GOD, "that My fury will mount up in

My anger. In My zeal and in My blazing wrath I declare that on that day there will surely be a great earthquake in the land of Israel. The fish of the sea, the birds of the heavens, the beasts of the field, all the creeping things that creep on the earth, and all the men who are on the face of the earth will shake at My presence; the mountains also will be thrown down, the steep pathways will collapse and every wall will fall to the ground. I will call for a sword against him on all My mountains," declares the Lord GOD. "Every man's sword will be against his brother. With pestilence and with blood I will enter into judgment with him; and I will rain on him and on his troops, and on the many peoples who are with him, a torrential rain, with hailstones, fire and brimstone. I will magnify Myself, sanctify Myself, and make Myself known in the sight of many nations; and they will know that I am the LORD." (38:18–22)

God is in absolute control of the entire situation. He will mount up in His fury to destroy these godless invaders. God will come to rescue His helpless, overwhelmed people using four means to totally destroy Russia and her Islamic allies.[31]

1. *A great earthquake* (see 38:19–20).

The Tribulation will be a time in which many terrible earthquakes occur (see Matthew 24:7). But this specific earthquake will be used by God to conquer and confuse these invaders.

2. *Infighting among the troops of the various nations* (see 38:21).

In the chaos after the powerful earthquake, the armies of each of the nations represented will turn against each other. Just think about it: The troops from the various invading nations will speak Russian, Farsi, Arabic, and Turkic languages. They will probably begin to kill anyone that they can't identify. This will be the largest case of death by friendly fire in human history.

3. *Disease* (see 38:22a).

Gog and his troops will experience a horrible, lethal plague that will add to the misery and devastation already inflicted.

4. *Torrential rain, hailstones, fire, and burning sulfur* (see 38:22b).

Just as God destroyed Sodom and Gomorrah, He will pour fire from heaven on the invading army.

These nations will come to Israel to take her land, but the only piece of land they will claim in Israel will be their burial plots (see Ezekiel 39:12). They will set out to bury Israel, but God will bury them.

A Quick Look at the Big Screen

At this point it might be good to step back briefly and take a look at how this invasion fits into God's overall prophetic program, to see how this one piece fits into the overall puzzle. The destruction of the vast horde of Islamic invaders in the days just before the middle of the tribulation period will serve at least two important purposes in God's prophetic master plan.

First, the destruction of this major bloc of nations (Russia and her Islamic allies) will pave the way for the Antichrist to establish his world kingdom with little resistance. There will be a dramatic shift in the balance of power in favor of the Antichrist, making him the undisputed leader of the world. After this battle ends, the Antichrist will seize this opportunity to break his seven-year covenant with Israel at the midpoint as predicted in Daniel 9:27 and begin his three-and-a-half-year reign of terror (see Revelation 13:5–7).

Second, this will not only pave the way for Antichrist's invasion of Israel and military rule of the world, but also prepare the world stage for his demand that all the world worship him as God (see 2 Thessalonians 2:3–4; Revelation 13:8). As long as Islam is a major force in the world, it is very difficult to imagine a one-world religion with one man worshiped as God.

Consider this: After the rapture of all true Christians to heaven, which of the major world religions would pose the greatest obstacle to Antichrist's demand to be worshiped? Islam. There are approximately one billion Muslims worldwide who would vehemently resist worshiping a man as God. But with the destruction of their armies in Israel by God, those who are left in the Islamic nations will be unable to mount much of a protest against Antichrist's demand that he be worshiped as God.

With the destruction of Russia and her Islamic allies, Antichrist will be able to put his program into full swing to rule the world militarily, economically, and religiously for three and a half years. Of course at the end of the three and a half years he too will be defeated in Israel at Armageddon when Jesus comes back to earth to establish His glorious kingdom on earth (see Revelation 16:16; 19:11–21).

PUTTING IT ALL TOGETHER

W. A. Criswell was one of the greatest pastors and preachers in American history. He pastored the First Baptist Church in Dallas for fifty years. Dr. Criswell also loved Bible prophecy. In his 1987 commentary on Ezekiel, he wrote these timely words concerning the prophecy of Ezekiel 38–39:

> The prophet Ezekiel lived 2,500 years ago and yet he writes as though he were a correspondent for the daily newspapers of the earth. What he says is so pertinent this moment that it is as though he lived in the places where history is unfolding before our very eyes.[32]

Ezekiel is God's war correspondent for today's newspapers. We have gone through his inspired prophecy in Ezekiel 38–39 with our Bibles in one hand and today's newspaper in the other. Here is what we have seen.

EZEKIEL'S PROPHECY: TODAY'S NEWSPAPER

Israel will be regathered to her land. This began in 1948 and continues up to this very moment. It is estimated that approximately 40 percent of the Jews in the world today are now back in Israel. In a few years half of the Jews in the world will be back in the land of Israel.

Israel will find temporary peace. The world has no option but to come up with some comprehensive peace plan for Israel and her neighbors, and the European Union is emerging more and more as a mediator in the peace talks just as the Bible predicts. The Antichrist will rise out of Europe, the reunited Roman empire, to bring peace (albeit temporarily) to Israel.

An alliance of nations from all sides will attack Israel in the end times. The nations listed in Ezekiel 38 are all

Islamic except Russia, and most have a common hatred for Israel. They would love nothing more than to launch an all-out attack against Israel while she is under a peace treaty with the West, thus making an attack on Israel also an attack on the West.

Knowing what God has predicted in His Word brings such clarity and focus to the world today, doesn't it? Think of it! The stage is being set right before our eyes. God's script is being followed to a tee. The jigsaw-puzzle picture on the top of the box is taking form. There is a remarkable correspondence between the trend of world events and what God predicted approximately 2,600 years ago in Ezekiel's prophecy.

So how should we respond? What is the proper response to such an incredible revelation?

KNOWING GOD

O ne of the problems people sometimes have
when they study Bible prophecy is knowing
how to apply what they have learned to their
lives. Sometimes people might think that since
prophecy deals with the future, it has no relation to
the present. But one of the great things about Ezekiel
38–39 is that God has not left us in the dark about
how He wants us to respond to the Battle of Gog and
Magog.

God says that the events of this great end-time
battle will happen that "they will know that I am the
LORD" (39:6, 7, 28). In fact, this statement that the

purpose of God's judgment was to cause Israel or the nations "to know that I am the LORD" is repeated over sixty-five times in Ezekiel.[33]

The purpose of the great prophecy of the Battle of Gog and Magog is to lead men and women to see the glory, majesty, and sovereignty of God so that they turn to Him and come to know who He really is. But how do we really get to know God?

HOW TO MEET GOD

Before we can get to know someone, what's the natural first step? We have to be introduced, don't we? It's the same in our relationship with God. The problem for us is that there is a barrier that keeps us away from God. There's a barrier that keeps us from ever even getting introduced to Him. And that barrier is our sin.

God's Word declares that all men are sinners, both by nature and by action (see Romans 3:23). The Bible also declares that God is infinitely holy, righteous, and just, and that he cannot accept sinners into His holy presence. As you can see right off, this is a major problem. How can a holy God accept sinful man? How can we possibly come into the presence of a holy God in our sinful condition?

God in His infinite wisdom and grace formulated a plan to remedy this problem. God the Son agreed to step out of eternity into time, to take on human flesh, to live the sinless life we could never live, and to die in our place. He took all our sins and took all the punishment we deserved. The full wrath of the Father, which should have been poured out on us, was instead heaped upon Jesus when He hung on the cross.

Just before He died, Jesus cried out "It is finished!" (John 19:30). The debt for your sins and mine was paid in full. Jesus paid it all. Now He wants to introduce you to His Father. He wants you to come to know God. But you have to come through Him! Jesus said, "I am the way, and the truth, and the life; no one comes to the Father but through Me" (John 14:6).

All that remains for you to have a relationship with this holy God forever is for you to personally receive as a free gift the full pardon Jesus has already purchased for you. Carefully read these words from Scripture, and ask God to make them clear in your heart and mind.

But as many as received Him, to them He gave the right to become children of God, even to those who believe in His name. (John 1:12)

For the wages of sin is death, but the free gift of God is eternal life in Christ Jesus our Lord. (Romans 6:23)

For by grace you have been saved through faith; and that not of yourselves, it is the gift of God; not as a result of works, so that no one may boast. (Ephesians 2:8–9)

You can receive Jesus Christ as your personal Savior right now as you read these words. God is offering you the free gift of eternal life. Don't wait. Receive the Savior now. Make sure you get to know God before it's too late. Take the free gift of pardon God is offering you. Call upon the Lord right now in prayer, and He will save you.

God's Word says that "Whoever will call on the name of the Lord will be saved" (Romans 10:13). It is the greatest decision you will ever make. When you trust Christ, you will immediately be introduced to God for the very first time. You will begin a relationship with God that will never end.

Why not pray a prayer something like this right now?

> *Father, I come to You now and admit that I'm a sinner. I know that I need a Savior. I acknowledge that I can never earn my own way to heaven. I accept Jesus as the Savior I need. I believe that He died and rose again for me. I receive the full pardon that He purchased for me on the cross. Thank You for saving me and allowing me to know You personally. Amen.*

GETTING BETTER ACQUAINTED

If you have just prayed that prayer or have been previously introduced to God by accepting Jesus Christ as your personal Savior, then as in any relationship, God wants you to get to know Him better. How do you get better acquainted with someone you have just met? It's really quite simple, isn't it? You talk to them and listen to them.

It's the same in our relationship with God. He wants you to talk to Him every day in prayer, to pour out your heart to Him in praise and petition. And then He wants to talk to you every day in His Word, the Bible. Begin reading God's Word every day and spending a few minutes in prayer. And also be sure to find a church home where God's Word is faithfully taught and where the people express the love of God. The Lord uses other people who know Him to help us to get to know Him better.

HOPE IN THIS HOUR

After World War II was over, the cold war began to set in, and the world entered the nuclear age. At that time the late Sir Winston Churchill asked a young American clergyman, "Young man, can you give me any hope?" Many today, as they look at our world, are asking the same question. The answer is a resounding yes!

And the hope for this world, for you and me, is a person: the Lord Jesus Christ.

The crucified, risen, and returning King of kings. He is our hope. He is the only hope.

Make sure you really know Him! That's why God gave us the great prophecy of the Battle of Gog and Magog: that you might "know that I am the LORD."

Get to know Him. As the prophet Amos said, "Prepare to meet your God" (Amos 4:12). His coming could be very soon.

It could be today!

The publisher and author would love to hear your comments about this book. *Please contact us at:* www.multnomah.net/hitchcock

NOTES

1. Fouad Ajami, "The Threat of Radical Islam," *Reader's Digest,* April 2002, 62.

2. Flavius Josephus, *Antiquities,* 1.6.1.

3. Ahmed Rashid, *Jihad: The Rise of Militant Islam in Central Asia* (New Haven, Conn.: Yale University Press, 2002), 8, 137–55.

4. Ibid., 9, 115–36.

5. Ibid., 4.

6. Imam Ibn Kathir, "The Appearance of Gog and Magog," *The Signs before the Day of Judgment.* http://www.kitaabun.co.uk (accessed May 9, 2002); Randall Price, *Unholy War* (Eugene, Ore.: Harvest

House Publishers, 2001), 310.

7. C. F. Keil, "Ezekiel, Daniel," in *Commentary on the Old Testament,* trans. James Martin (reprint, Grand Rapids, Mich.: Eerdmans Publishing Company, 1982), 9:159; Wilhelm Gesenius, *Gesenius' Hebrew-Chaldee Lexicon to the Old Testament,* trans. Samuel Prideaux Tregelles (Grand Rapids, Mich.: Eerdmans Publishing Company, 1949), 752.

8. Gesenius, *Gesenius' Hebrew-Chaldee Lexicon,* 26.

9. "The World Factbook 2001" *Central Intelligence Agency,* http://www.cia.gov/cia/publications/factbook/index.html (accessed May 24, 2002).

10. Rashid, *Jihad,* 235.

11. C. I. Scofield, ed., *The Scofield Study Bible* (New York: Oxford University Press, 1909), 883.

12. Ralph H. Alexander, "Ezekiel," in *The Expositor's Bible Commentary,* ed. Frank E. Gaebelein, (Grand Rapids, Mich.: Zondervan Publishing Company, 1986), 6:930.

13. Nicole Pope and Hugh Pope, *Turkey Unveiled: A History of Modern Turkey* (Woodstock, N.Y.: The Overlook Press, 1997), 316.

14. Ibid., 330–31.

15. Benjamin Netanyahu, *Fighting Terrorism,* (New York: Farrar, Straus and Giroux, 2001), 91–3.

16. Pope, *Turkey Unveiled,* 317.

17. Ibid., 316.

18. Netanyahu, *Fighting Terrorism,* 122–23.

19. Ibid., 79.

20. Syed Saleem Shahzad, "Iran Takes Center Stage." *Asia Times Online,* 22 January 2002. http://www.atimes.com/c-asia/DA22Ag01.html (accessed May 7, 2002).

21. Gilles Kepel, *Jihad: The Trail of Political Islam,* trans. Anthony F. Roberts (Cambridge, Mass.: The Belnap Press, 2002), 184.

22. Both Gesenius (Gesenius, *Gesenius' Hebrew-Chaldee Lexicon,* 668) and Brown (Francis Brown, *The New Brown-Driver-Briggs-Gesenius Hebrew and English Lexicon,* [Peabody, Mass.: Hendrickson Publishers, 1979], 806) identify Put as Libya. Also, in the Septuagint, the Greek translation of the Old Testament, Put is translated *Libues.*

23. Those who argue that this invasion was ful-filled at some point in the past face the insurmountable

obstacle of showing when anything even remotely similar to this ever occurred in Israel's history.

24. Some scholars see the references to horses, swords, shields, and bows and arrows in Ezekiel 38–39 as indicative of ancient warfare, not a battle in the twenty-first century. However, this is not a great problem in that biblical prophets could easily be speaking of warfare in the distant future using descriptions of weaponry and tactics that would be familiar to them and their original audience.

25. Those who place this invasion at the end of the Millennium point to Revelation 20:7–9, which is the only other reference in the Bible to "Gog and Magog." The problem is that the invasion of Gog and Magog in Revelation occurs after the Millennium described in Revelation 20:1–6, whereas in Ezekiel 38–39, the Battle of Gog and Magog occurs before Ezekiel's description of the millennial reign of Christ in Ezekiel 40–48. In other words, Ezekiel's Battle of Gog and Magog is before the Millennium, or premillennial, while John's is postmillennial. They are separated by over one thousand years. So the question naturally arises is this: If they aren't talking about the

same invasion, how do we explain John's use of "Gog and Magog" in Revelation 20:7–9? Why does he borrow this language from Ezekiel? I believe the best answer is that John is using this phrase as a kind of shorthand to communicate to his readers what this battle will be like, just as today we might use the term *Waterloo* to describe a disastrous defeat. John is saying that at the end of the Millennium there will be another Battle of Gog and Magog when a vast confederation of nations comes against Israel and is destroyed by the judgment of God. Using this simple phrase saves him from having to describe it in further detail.

26. R. Laird Harris, Gleason L. Archer, and Bruce K. Waltke, eds. *Theological Wordbook of the Old Testament* (Chicago: Moody Press, 1980), 1:101.

27. John F. Walvoord, *The Nations in Prophecy* (Grand Rapids, Mich.: Zondervan Publishing House, 1967), 115.

28. For an excellent presentation of this view of the timing, see J. Dwight Pentecost, "Where Do the Events of Ezekiel 38–39 Fit into the Prophetic Picture," *Bibliotheca Sacra* 114 (October 1957): 334–46.

29. Billy Graham, *Approaching Hoofbeats: The Four Horsemen of the Apocalypse* (Waco, Tex.: Word Books, 1983), 122–23.

30. Brown, *Hebrew and English Lexicon*, 1076; Gesenius, *Gesenius' Hebrew-Chaldee Lexicon*, 875.

31. In Ezekiel 39:2, the King James Version reads as if only five-sixths of the invading army will be destroyed. "And I will turn thee back, and *leave but the sixth part of thee*" (emphasis added). However, most modern versions translate the Hebrew verb as "lead thee on" (ASV), "drive you on" (NASB), "drag you along" (NIV), and "drive you" (NLT). These translations are preferred over the King James Version. See Charles Lee Feinberg, *The Prophecy of Ezekiel* (Chicago: Moody Press, 1969), 228.

32. W. A. Criswell, *Expository Sermons on the Book of Ezekiel* (Grand Rapids, Mich.: Zondervan Publishing House, 1987), 212.

33. Alexander, *The Expositor's Bible Commentary*, 6:746.

Hitchcock Examines Bible Prophecy's Silence About America

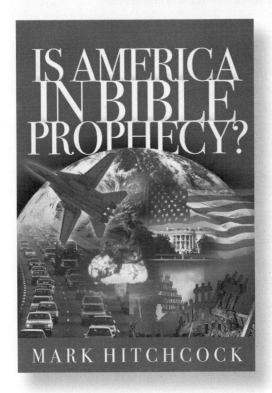

"If you have questions about the end times, you will find the answers in these books."

—DR. TIMOTHY LAHAYE

In *Is America in Bible Prophecy?*, expert Mark Hitchcock deals with often-raised questions about America's future. Examining three prophetic passages that are commonly thought to describe America, Hitchcock concludes that the Bible is actually silent about the role of the United States in the end times. He then discusses the implications of America's absence in prophetic writings. Along with Hitchcock's compelling forecast for the future, he offers specific actions Americans can take to keep their nation strong and blessed by God, as well as an appendix of additional questions and answers.

ISBN 1-57673-496-X

What's your biggest worry about end times?

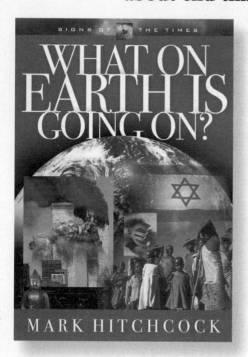

> "Hitchcock demonstrates unusual skill in interpreting the prophetic Scriptures."
>
> —J. DWIGHT PENECOST,
> Professor emeritus of Bible Exposition,
> Dallas Theological Seminary

As sensationalists and skeptics wreak havoc with the country's emotions, prophecy expert Mark Hitchcock provides a much-needed definition of what is meant by signs of the times. In *What on Earth Is Going On?*, Hitchcock discusses the current interest in prophecy caused by the 9/11 attack, presents Jesus' own forecast for the future of the world, and details five major global developments today that discernibly signal Christ's coming. This balanced, concise overview of the real signs of the times will clarify Christ's instructions challenging His followers to be alert in the final days. Readers will easily find and absorb the information they need to prepare for His return.

ISBN 1-57673-853-1

"The End Is Near!"

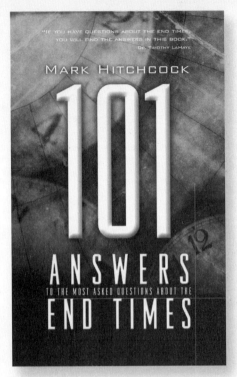

"If you have questions about the end times, you will find the answers in this book."
—DR. TIMOTHY LAHAYE

MARK HITCHCOCK

101

ANSWERS

TO THE MOST ASKED QUESTIONS ABOUT THE

END TIMES

"Mark's book fills a real need in the study of prophecy. Finally, there's one book that gives solid, biblical answers to all the key questions that people today are asking about the end times."

—DR. TIMOTHY LAHAYE

Or is it? The Antichrist is alive and well today! *Or is he?* The church is about to be raptured and will certainly escape the Tribulation…*right?* When it comes to the end times, there's so much confusion. Preachers with elaborate charts share their theories about Revelation and other prophetic books of the Bible. "Ah, Babylon stands for the United States," they say. But then other teachers share their theories: "No, Babylon stands for the Roman Catholic Church, or the European Union, or the literal Babylon rebuilt in Iraq…." *Would somebody please shoot straight with me?* Finally, someone has. Gifted scholar and pastor Mark Hitchcock walks you gently through Bible prophecy in an engaging, user-friendly style. Hitchcock's careful examination of the topic will leave you feeling informed and balanced in your understanding of events to come…in our time?

ISBN 1-57673-952-X